HOLIDAYS AND FESTIVALS

Election Day

Rebecca Rissman

Heinemann Library
Chicago, Illinois

www.heinemannraintree.com

Visit our website to find out more information about Heinemann-Raintree books.

To order:

☎ Phone 888-454-2279

⌨ Visit www.heinemannraintree.com to browse our catalog and order online.

Edited by Adrian Vigliano and Rebecca Rissman
Designed by Ryan Frieson
Picture research by Tracy Cummins
Leveling by Nancy E. Harris
Originated by Capstone Global Library Ltd.
Printed in China by South China Printing Company Ltd.

15 14 13 12 11 10
10 9 8 7 6 5 4 3 2 1

Library of Congress Cataloging-in-Publication Data
Rissman, Rebecca.
  Election Day / Rebecca Rissman.
     p. cm.—(Holidays and festivals)
  Includes bibliographical references and index.
  ISBN 978-1-4329-4063-8 (hc)—ISBN 978-1-4329-4082-9 (pb) 1. Election Day—Juvenile literature. 2. Elections—United States—Juvenile literature. I. Title.
  JK1978.R57 2011
  324.973—dc22
                                          2009052906

Acknowledgments

The author and publishers are grateful to the following for permission to reproduce copyright material: Corbis ©BRENDAN MCDERMID/Reuters **p.5**; Corbis ©Bettmann **p.9**; Corbis ©Jeff Haynes/Pool/CNP **p.15**; Corbis ©Carlos Barria/Reuters **p.17**; Corbis ©Max Whittaker **p.19**; Corbis ©Guy Reynolds/Dallas Morning News **pp.20**, **23**; Getty Images/Hola Images **p.4**; Getty Images/William Barnes Wollen **p.8**; Getty Images/Mario Tama **p.14**; Getty Images/Marc Serota **p.16**; istockphoto ©narvikk **p.21**; istockphoto ©John Clines **p.22**; Library of Congress Prints and Photographs Division **p.18**; Shutterstock ©Victorian Traditions **p.13**; The Granger Collection, New York **pp.6**, **10**, **11**, **12**.

Cover photograph of American voting pins reproduced with permission of Getty Images/Comstock. Back cover photograph reproduced with permission of istockphoto ©narvikk.

Every effort has been made to contact copyright holders of any material reproduced in this book. Any omissions will be rectified in subsequent printings if notice is given to the publisher.

Contents

What Is a Holiday?

People celebrate holidays.
A holiday is a special day.

Election Day is a holiday. Election Day happens every other November.

The Story of Election Day

Long ago many people left England. They moved to the American colonies.

6

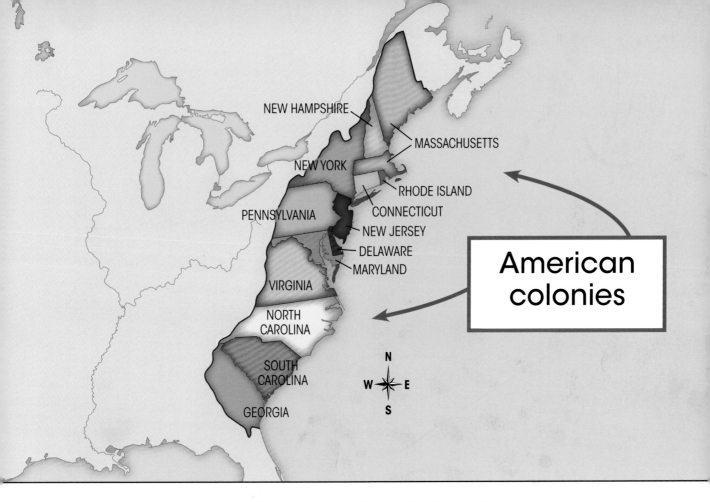

They were called colonists. The colonists were ruled by the King of England.

The colonists wanted to start their own country. They fought England to become free.

The United States of America became a country. The Americans formed a government called a democracy.

In a democracy, people choose who will be their leader.

In a democracy, people vote for what they want.

In 1788 Americans voted for the first time.

They voted to make George
Washington the president. The president
is the leader of the United States.

Celebrating Election Day

Every two years, people come together on Election Day.

People vote for a president every four years on Election Day.

People vote to choose other leaders on Election Day.

People decide what they want for their country.

Who Can Vote?

Long ago, not everyone could vote.
Women and black Americans could
not vote.

Today almost all Americans who are older than 18 can vote.

Election Day Symbols

The ballot is a symbol of Election Day. Ballots are tickets used to vote.

The American flag is a symbol of Election Day. It reminds people to be grateful that they can vote.

Calendar

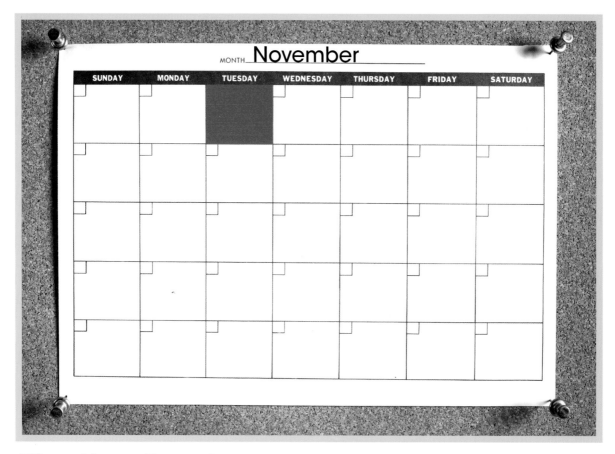

MONTH November

SUNDAY	MONDAY	TUESDAY	WEDNESDAY	THURSDAY	FRIDAY	SATURDAY

Election Day is every other November. It is on the first Tuesday after the first Monday of the month.

Picture Glossary

ballot the type of ticket used for voting

Index

Note to Parents and Teachers

Before reading

Ask the children what they know about voting. Have they seen adults vote? Have they ever voted (even if it's just by raising hands in class). Explain that America is a country where government officials are voted into office and that the day on which people vote is called Election Day.

After reading

Pick an activity on which to vote – which book for a read-aloud, what food for a special snack, etc. Make a ballot box and have the children write their vote on a slip of paper. Tally the votes as a group and may the most votes win!